# The Passion and the Paycheck

## Your Keys to Happiness and Success at Work

Serena Williamson, PhD

# The Passion and the Paycheck


info@SerenaWilliamson.com

Published by Book Coach Press
Ottawa ON, Canada
www.BookCoachPress.com
info@bookcoachpress.com



**Printed and Bound in Canada**
*Second Printing, 2008*

Design: Donald Lanouette
Editing: Karen Opas Lanouette

Library and Archives Canada Cataloguing in Publication

Williamson, Serena,
The passion and the paycheck / Serena Williamson.

**ISBN 978-0-9783066-6-3**

1. Psychology, Industrial. 2. Self-actualization (Psychology).
I. Title.
HF5548.8.W538 200 158.7 C2007-905962-7

The Passion and The Paycheck is neatly packaged — 35 vital strategies you can use to re-energize yourself at work — with lots of practical advice not found in similar books.

*Harvey Schachter*
*Managing Books columnist,*
*Globe and Mail*

This book is fun and quick to read. I found the multiple anecdotes and analogies to be an amazing collection of truths that are very easy to understand. It really does bring together all the pieces needed to unlock one's own possibilities. This is the kind of book that I can imagine will be bought by executives to be distributed to employees who really want to move forward in life, both personally and professionally.

*David Booker*
*Chief Operating Officer,*
*Learning Tree International*

# *TABLE OF CONTENTS*

## TABLE OF CONTENTS

# Introduction

*The Passion and the Paycheck* provides refreshing and concrete strategies that you and your people can use to reduce stress, find encouragement, stay on track, and keep moving forward.

Any one of these strategies can make your day. Collectively, they can change your life.

This book contains wisdom gained through leading, advising, coaching, counselling, and training many thousands of people from all walks of life over the past twenty years.

*The Passion and the Paycheck*'s thirty-five strategies come alive with true stories of people who have struggled with the same issues you have, and the handy checklist at the end of each chapter brings these strategies home.

We hope that you and your people will use what you learn from *The Passion and the Paycheck,* in addition to what you already know, and that you will find yourselves less stressed, encouraged, back on track, and moving forward.

# KNOW YOURSELF

***And the day came when the risk it took to remain tightly closed in a bud was more painful than the risk it took to bloom.***

Anaïs Nin

## Stop, Look, and Listen

***If the passion has gone out of your paycheck—if you are stressed-out, unhappy, discouraged, or off-track, you can do something about it. First, you must take the time to figure out what is going on. Only then can you take constructive action and get back on track again.***

The need to stop, look, and listen caught Marie by surprise one day. She was coming out of a meeting when a colleague approached her and said, "Marie, what's the matter with you? You're a shadow of your former self. You seem to have lost your zest." His comment caught her off guard. She thought she had been hiding it better than that.

She had been working hard, putting in extra hours on a variety of projects, but ironically, the same day she received a complimentary letter from the company president, she was saying to herself, "I can't do this job anymore. It's killing me. I'm going to be somewhere else next year."

She had gotten so caught up in the day-to-day, that she was on a treadmill. In truth, she was miserable, but hadn't had the time even to admit it to herself, let alone decide what to do.

If there is even a part of you that feels like Marie felt, perhaps it is time to stop, take a few deep breaths and figure out what is going on.

When people start to experience that restlessness, statistics often show that they are losing their sense of mission. They had begun their job with a conviction that they could make a difference. When that began to get lost in the daily tasks of getting the job done, they continued to bring their brains to the job, but they did not bring their zest.

When asked about their sense of mission, people sometimes get nervous. *Mission* is such an important-sounding word that they think it is only for important people like Martin Luther King or Mother Theresa.

Mother Theresa was not born with the mission to work with the poorest of the poor. Martin Luther King did not know as a child that he would lead people to freedoms they had only dreamed of. These leaders rose because they noticed what was going on around them and made the decision to *do* something about it.

The first step in rediscovering your sense of mission is to behave as you would at a railway crossing. Stop, look, and listen. Take a quiet time each day, if only for a few minutes, and take some deep breaths. If you have more time, go for a run, play a game of tennis, or work in your garden. Do whatever you need to do to give yourself some time for reflection. Ask the questions, "Who am I and what am I here for?" and see what comes to you.

Do this without judgment, fear or concern. Just notice. And don't leap to any conclusions. Watch and listen, both to yourself and to those around you. You will be amazed at what you will see and hear when you pay attention and don't rush to solutions too quickly.

To guide your reflection, try using the three magic keys described in the next section.

## Three Magic Keys

***What are you good at? What do you love? What does the world need?***

When looking for your mission at work; that is, what fires your engine, there are three magic keys. The keys are three questions you must ask yourself. Originally developed by Richard Bolles, these questions form the basis of all career management programs. Rather than taking the minimum three months these programs require, use these two pages for the quick and easy shortcut.

The first question is: "What are my special gifts," or "What am I good at?" What do you do best? What are your talents and skills? Make a list. Even if you think they are not unique or special, just jot down what comes to your mind first. Are you a good carpenter, a great organizer, a network specialist, a programmer, a creative writer, or a talented manager? What are you good at?

The second question is: What do you love doing? Make a second list. What puts a smile on your face and gives you a sense of satisfaction? Do you love helping people? Do you love being creative? Do you love solving problems or fixing things? It is okay if some of the same things are on both lists. That is the main idea, actually. You are looking for both what you are good at and what you love doing.

The third question is more complex and perhaps difficult to answer at first. It is: "What does the world need?"

We can all agree that the world needs many things such as peace, sufficient food, and homes for all. So this question can seem quite intimidating. A simpler way to ask this question is: "What difference can *I* make? What difference *do I want* to make? What can I do in my corner of the world, in my career, right now?"

Once you have made your three lists, circle the key words and underline the duplicates. Then fill in the blanks below:

I am great at______________________________________

I love ____________________________________________

The difference I want to make is____________________

___________________________________________________

___________________________________________________

___________________________________________________

Often our three keys are right in front of us, but we do not see them because we are looking for something that is more complicated.

Joe, the union representative attending a seminar, answered these key questions with: "I love fixing things, I am a great mechanic, and I am good at leading people. The difference I want to make is to get more money for the mechanics." He got a laugh from the audience when he said this, but sometimes the truest words are said in jest. He is now president of his union and involved in getting the government to change its legislation so his people can have wage increases. He is doing his part to make *his* world a better place. And the many mechanics that he represents are enormously grateful. They do not need a Gandhi or Florence Nightingale. They need Joe.

## Listen to Your Body

***Often the body gets messages before the mind does. Pay attention to your body's signals. Both positive and negative signs can indicate where your passion lies and provide career direction.***

Research has shown us the connection between stress and illness. We know stress can lead to heart attack and stroke, and that it can depress the immune system. What we forget is that, by listening to our body, we can play a part in our own wellness.

Think about your own work life. Certain people and tasks give you energy while other people and tasks drain you. Pay attention.

Marie was accomplishing great things in her job but she was tired all the time. Jared was a valued employee, but having to manage people instead of being creative was draining him. When they stopped and paid attention, they were able to come up with solutions.

Let's play this out in your life. Think of the last time you got sick. What was going on in your life just before you crawled into bed and pulled the covers over your head? I'll bet you the price of this book that you were overwhelmed about something. Getting sick was a giant stop sign. It caught your attention. Write that down, and put a skull and crossbones beside it.

On the positive side, think of a time when you felt really great at work. What was going on? What were you doing? Who were you doing it with? Write that down, and put check marks there.

Which people in your life give you energy? List a few. After spending time with these people, you always feel great. Write down how you feel when you are with them. What happens to you—to your face, your body, even your heart rate?

What is it about these positive people that you like? What are their qualities? These are the kinds of people with whom you need to surround yourself.

In summary, paying attention to the signals your body gives you—mentally, emotionally, and physically—will give you direction. Making sincere attempts to avoid, as much as possible, the people and tasks that make you feel ill and filling your life with people and tasks that make you feel great is a powerful tool to put the passion back into your paycheck. Being realistic, all projects have both. The key here is to pay attention and do your best to choose where you spend your time.

## Be Open to New Possibilities

***Sometimes answers come in ways we were not expecting. Don't throw an idea in the trash just because it is different. Explore it first. You may find surprising solutions.***

Louise had been working in the same policy unit with the same people for years. She was good at her job, but she was bored. She knew she was capable of handling much more responsibility than she currently had. But she loved her organization and didn't want to leave.

Then one day a colleague told her of an opening in a different division of her organization, a division that Louise held in very high regard. Indeed, it had been Louise's secret dream to work there, but she didn't dare even entertain the thought. It was a small unit with a chief and three employees, but this unit was Counselling Services and it provided advice and direction not only to thirteen psychologists across the country but also to all 24,000 of the organization's employees, from administrative support to senior managers. The woman Louise was looking to replace had a PhD. Louise had a high school education. Louise screwed up her courage and made an appointment to talk with the chief.

Louise did not even have her resume with her. Why waste time polishing it up if there was no hope? She just went to gather information.

During the conversation, Louise and the chief developed great rapport. Although Louise did not have the paper credentials, she had research experience, which the chief required, and was a creative, innovative self-starter, which the chief also required. She was committed to the organization, admired the work the unit was doing, and was prepared to work hard to fill any gaps in her learning.

The chief said she was interested in taking the matter further—if Louise thought she could do the job—and asked for Louise's resume. Louise said she would bring it to her the following morning.

That evening, Louise polished up her resume, emphasizing what she and the chief had discussed. The next day she handed it in and two weeks later she started her new job, in the unit of her dreams, with a boss she admired. The PhD moved on to work that suited her much better and the chief was thrilled to have someone on board who really wanted to be there.

Don't let your presuppositions stop you. The rules are defined by the exceptions every day. If Louise's courage could change the rules, so can yours. It's only impossible if you do not try.

By the way, Louise's story may sound too good to be true. It isn't. Louise is her real name. I know because I was the chief.

## Engage Your Whole Brain

***Learn to use both sides of your brain at work. Instead of sapping the energy from the rational left side of your brain, keep mental energy at its peak by using the creative right half, too.***

Brain research has taught us that the two hemispheres of the brain function quite differently from each other. The left side controls the logical, rational functions while the right side controls the more creative, intuitive functions. At work, we have learned to draw mostly on the logical left hemisphere. Since many of us strive to get more done each day and handle increasing numbers of projects at once, we are putting a lot of stress on one side of our brain.

The irony is that many people, even while working ten or twelve-hour days and being somewhat stressed, believe they are capable of achieving more than their job requires. That desire for "more" is clearly not about quantity, it is about quality. It is the thirst to use the creative side of the brain. Jared's situation is a prime example.

Jared is a technology expert. He was doing so well at work that he was declared a "valuable asset" during a major corporate merger that saw many people lose their jobs. He was soon promoted to manager of his unit and given a raise. Six months later a small start-up contacted him, and he considered leaving his current company to go join them.

Why would Jared, such a valued employee, consider leaving? He was feeling bored and unchallenged. The heart of the matter was that he did not want to be a manager; he wanted to be creative. Even though the new company's salary promises were sketchy and he had a young family to support, Jared was thrilled at the possibility of being on the leading edge. The left side of Jared's brain was exhausted but his right brain was bursting with energy.

Jared went to have a conversation with his boss, effectively to give notice that he was leaving. The boss was disappointed, but, thankfully, he was a quick thinker and a good listener. He asked Jared why he was looking to leave and paid attention to the answer. The boss then offered Jared the opportunity to open a creative department at his own company. Jared gratefully accepted the offer. It has been three years and he is still happily there.

So how does this apply to you? Are you using both sides of your brain at work? Creativity is not restricted to artists and poets. We all have right sides to our brains. We are being creative when we look at things from new angles, when we are willing to entertain new ideas.

Engaging the right side of the brain fuels our energy both mentally and physically. Let ideas run free in you mind and jot them down, dictate them into a recorder, or doodle something to represent them before they fly away. Don't worry; you do not have to take action on everything that comes into your head right now.

As you develop the right side of your brain, your ideas will begin to take shape and point clearly at the direction in which you need to go. You may end up doing your current job differently or, like Jared, you may find something else in your organization that inspires you more.

You will enjoy your work far more, have more energy, and be a much greater asset to your organization, when the creative right side of your brain is engaged too.

## Reconnect With Your Wisdom

***Once you are clear on what you love doing best at work, you will not be satisfied with less. Remember why you chose your job in the first place. It required talents and skills that you enjoyed using and satisfied your need to make a difference. Reconnect with the wisdom of your choices.***

Sue was up early one morning when she heard the sound of trucks, realized it was recycling day, and scrambled outside, boxes in hand. What happened next is an exquisite example of reconnecting with the wisdom of your choices.

Sue lives in an area that, although near the center of a large city, has a fun village-like feeling. There is a corner hardware store, pharmacy, pizza place, and greasy spoon. As she dropped the recycling boxes at the curb, her eye caught something different in the lane beside the ice cream parlor. She thought she saw directors' chairs where cars should be. She went to investigate.

Thin, tanned people with headsets were rushing about carrying changes of clothes on hangers, and disappearing into the local retirement home. A professionally made-up young woman carrying a clipboard seemed to be in charge of something, so Sue asked her what was going on.

The women told Sue that a film starring the actress Janeane Garofalo was being produced for Lifetime Channel.

"Wow!" Sue thought, "What fun. I have never watched a film being produced. If I stand here and watch long enough, maybe they will ask me to be in it." She did and they did! So she scrambled into her house to grab a few wardrobe changes and, head high in pride and anticipation, carried her clothing into the retirement home, whose lounge had been magically transformed into the "extras" holding room.

She spent the day chatting with other extras, then changing clothes and walking back and forth when they told her to. They liked the yellow tee shirt she had thrown on to take out the garbage (go figure!) so they gave her a special scene in which Janeane Garofalo and Sue bump into each other in the greasy spoon's foyer. She was having fun and loving it, until about three in the afternoon.

She was having a blast, but she was also starting to get a little bored. Although she had dreamed of being in the movies, as many of us have, she understood why she had never pursued it as a career. It was fun, inspiring, and uplifting for a short while, but it did not sustain her interest and sense of making a difference. The next day, Sue found that she returned to her job with renewed enthusiasm; not only because she had had the fun of the distraction and the excitement of being in a Hollywood movie, but also because she realized how much she preferred her own job.

So how does story this apply to you at work? We all make many choices in our lives. If you chose your current career and job, it was certainly for more than money. It always is. If you are saying to yourself, "Why did I go into this career? Why didn't I ______________?" perhaps you chose to do what you are doing because something about it turned you on; and you didn't choose the other, even if you may have been good at it, because something about it turned you off.

What is it about your work that is meaningful and satisfying to you? What is it about your specific skills and talents that you enjoy using? Reconnecting with that can put the smile back on your face and the spring in your step. If perhaps your job has changed and you are no longer doing what it was you joined the company for in the first place, maybe you need to give that some thought and, in time, have a serious conversation with your boss about what you could do about it. If you have changed and now want to do different things, that is okay too.

And by the way, don't forget to have some fun times. You may not get to be in the movies like Sue, but you do have hobbies that fuel your soul. Remember to include them in your life to keep you refreshed and enthusiastic.

## Passion Action Checklist

- ❑ I have taken the time to stop and reflect on what may be missing for me at work, and what might make me more enthusiastic.

- ❑ I have identified what I am good at, what I love, and what I think the world needs from me and encapsulated it into one sentence.

- ❑ I am paying attention to the signals I get from my body and going with the positive.

- ❑ I am keeping my mind open to new ideas.

- ❑ I am using both sides of my brain.

- ❑ I remember why I chose this job in the first place.

# GET YOURSELF OUT OF YOUR WAY

***People in distress will sometimes prefer a problem that is familiar to a solution that is not.***

Neil Postman

## Shed the Snakeskin

***As the snake grows, it has to break out of its old skin and leave it behind. To revitalize your spirit, you need to be like the snake and let go of any beliefs, attitudes, and perspectives that do not serve you any longer and learn to see yourself in a new way.***

Now that you have taken some time to figure out what you want to do at work, it is time to get any stumbling blocks out of the way so you can move forward. The first and foremost of these is the way you see yourself and your place in the world.

Often people's belief systems no longer serve them, yet they cling to them. To clarify, let us look at a common example.

Information technology professionals often do not see themselves as "people" people. Then they get promoted and suddenly find themselves working as managers. So they take courses on communication and leadership and discover a wealth of information that they never even knew existed. It seems as if they have touched the tip of a vast iceberg of information. How could they ever learn it all?

Beginning to take in this vastly different body of information involves a bit of a leap. They have to let go of being the engineer—the professional who knew it all—to someone who is just learning. They also have to go from being someone who did not really care about communication and people issues to seeing their value.

An important thing to remember here is that the snake that shed its skin is still the same snake, just bigger. So it is with the IT professional turned people manager. He or she has not stopped being an engineer, just added a new skill set to the existing one. It is the perspective that people cling to, the belief that they are technical specialists and not good with people, that can hold them back and keep the information from sinking in.

So how does this apply to you? Do you have an old perspective of yourself that is not working? Perhaps you see yourself as powerless, as a victim of corporate circumstances. Are you really? Maybe you need to shed that image, and instead of looking at what you cannot do, look at what you can. You are already doing something—you are reading this.

Perhaps you see yourself as a mom first and worker second, but now your children are grown and you could use work that is more exciting.

Perhaps you see yourself as a "hard worker" and you are getting exhausted and burned out. Maybe you need to shed the perspective of yourself as "hard worker" and change it to "wise worker."

Take a few minutes and think about how you see yourself at work. See whether you can find an old perspective or two that you can leave behind as the new you emerges.

## Don't Be Afraid to Switch

***Jobs can lose their luster. So be it. Just because you loved your career before doesn't mean you have to love it forever. It's okay to let go of old decisions and switch to something that will bring passion back into your paycheck.***

It is not necessary to cling to a career choice just because you were passionate about it years ago. Most people are excited about new jobs when they start. There may be some nervousness, but there is also enthusiasm and hope. After a while, however, the "honeymoon" wears off and the work can become routine. Still later, the work may seem downright dreadful.

The first step in dealing with this situation is to not beat yourself up for having chosen the career in the first place. People often do that. They expect themselves to have been able to predict the future. Guilt only compounds the problem.

You did not wake up one day and say to yourself, "I am going to make stupid decisions today." You selected your career, and accepted your current job, using all of the information available to you at the time. Now both you and the situation are different. It is not an admission of failure to want a change. People make many career shifts during their lives, and they can often do so within their current company. The key is to not let fear or guilt stop you.

You remember Jared from a previous story. Three years ago he switched jobs because he wanted to be creative.

Jared made friends' heads spin the other day when he told them that he is getting promoted and moving up to the management level. "But we thought you hated managing people, they exclaimed." "No," said Jared, "I don't dislike managing people, as a matter of fact I am quite looking forward to it." Jared's friends crinkled their eyes in disbelief and teased him a little, but he stuck to his story and did not get off track. Believe it or not, this is a true story. Three years later, Jared is really excited about the possibility of managing a group of people and is not ashamed to say so. Jared let himself change and did not make a fuss about it.

Have the courage to be like Jared. With experience and time, you are changing too. Having new interests today does not mean you were wrong yesterday. If you are reading this book, it is because you are looking for ways to put passion back into your paycheck. To do this, you have to let go not only of old perspectives, but also of old dreams. At one time you may have dreamed of having your current job. Now, you are developing new dreams and new visions of what you want to do with your career. To do that, you need to switch and let the old dreams go.

## Own the Good Stuff

***Listen to the good things people say about you and take pride in your accomplishments. If you are a perfectionist who thinks you are never good enough, it's time to let that go and get it out of your way.***

It is interesting that people often receive negative comments more easily than they do positive ones. People can find compliments both embarrassing and unbelievable. This is another factor from inside people's own minds, which can cause stress and diminish passion.

People all talk to themselves, but *eighty percent* of self-talk is negative. There is a built-in self-critic that may have developed early in life, which is always on the lookout for faults. The "perfectionist" has a particularly active self-critic. If you have trouble hearing the good stuff about yourself, let this book jolt you out of it. You don't have to be conceited, just take honest, balanced pride in your accomplishments.

If perfectionism is a challenge for you, you may be saying, "Yeah, that's easy for her to say. If I could have dropped it easily, I would have done so years ago."

If you believe your problem is very deeply seated, you could see a psychotherapist, but if you prefer, you can take a behavioural approach and deal with it yourself. You can train your self-critic to sit down and be quiet. Every time you hear yourself say something negative to yourself, look for the grain of truth, fix it, and move on. Don't dwell on it. You can visit "Pity City", but don't move in!

If the self-critic brings up something you can learn from, it can be helpful to your career. If, however, you are using this information to beat yourself up, stop! Mentally tell your self-critic to go sit in a corner for a while and be quiet. Create an image of your self-critic that makes it smaller and reduces its power. Turn it into an ant.

On the other side of the coin, learn to receive compliments rather than thinking "Yeah, but..." and finishing the compliment with some mental criticism either of yourself or of the person who complimented you. Train yourself to receive the compliment gracefully. Smile, say "Thank you," let yourself feel good for a few minutes, and savor that feeling. You are training both your mind and your body to feel good about yourself. This is not vanity, false pride, or any of the other negative words that we may have learned as children.

The energy that is created when you feel good about what you are doing diminishes your stress, feeds your positive self-image and supports you as you take the steps you need to get on track and put passion back into your paycheck.

## If Not Now, When?

***The time to take action is now; take baby steps or giant steps, but do something! People often procrastinate because the task seems scary. Take a deep breath. Break that scary task into manageable chunks, and take a bite.***

One of the most common complaints of people who are off track at work is that they have no time to reflect on what to do. They are just too busy.

We can learn a valuable lesson about time from Scott. Scott was unhappy at work. The lease was also up on his car. Scott complained that he had no time to think about what he wanted or to look within his current organization to see if there were other opportunities. He also had no time to network and no time to redo his resume. And because he had no new resume, be could not reply to any of the ads he saw on company bulletin boards, even if he *did* find them. And he needed a new car.

One day, Scott shared his problem with a friend at work. The friend suggested that Scott break the task into manageable chunks and take *two steps every day* toward finding his new car. Scott listened.

In the evenings he scanned magazines and newspapers for information on the latest vehicles. He read consumers reports, visited car dealerships and compared price on various models. Should he get one of those big sports utility vehicles since, after all, he did have a big dog that traveled with him? Or should he get another sedan? Should he go for the gusto and spend $850 a month on a luxury model or should he save his money and buy some new furniture instead? After over a month of evenings and weekends, Scott had enough information to make the decision and he leased a great new car. But he was still unhappy in his job. And he thought he had no time to do anything about it.

Then he realized he could do the same thing as he had done with finding a new car. He could *take two steps each day*. He changed his screen saver at work to a simple banner that read: "Two things."

And Scott took those two daily steps. Within six months, he was back on track. This was good for him and for his company. He got to do what he enjoyed, and his company got a more productive employee.

What are two things you could do today to move you closer to what you need to do to bring passion back into your paycheck? What are two things that would move your career into the direction you want?

And what two things could you do tomorrow?

Reading this book is the inspiration, but your taking action is what will make your goals, and attaining them, real.

## One Change at a Time

***As you move toward getting your career back on track, remember that change can be unsettling. Do your best to make only one major change at a time, and give yourself a period of time for adjustment.***

If you get a promotion and are moved to a new city, clearly you are going to have to adjust to many changes at once—new job, new home, new neighbors, new commute—to name a few. These changes cannot be avoided. But when you have a choice, it is far better to tackle only one big change at a time.

Most tables have four legs. If you think of your life as a table, you will fare much better if you don't loosen all the legs at once. If you change your job, move, and leave your marriage all at the same time, like the table, you could fall down. Keep as much of the rest of your life as stable as you can while you make a major career decision.

If your marriage is rocky, get some help before you make a major career shift. If you are contemplating taking on new responsibilities at work, this may not be the time to leave your wife.

People often think that a positive change will relieve stress. It may, but it will still involve a period of adjustment.

Since this book focuses on putting passion back into your career, that is where the majority of your energy should be going right now. Simmer everything else down for a little while. Don't buy that summer home just yet. Wait on the new car. Don't buy that big house. There will most likely be another house available when you have your career back on track. If you can, do only one major change at a time.

There is another aspect to making multiple changes at once that can come into play here. There is something about ending one thing and starting another that many people find scary. People in distress will often prefer a problem that is familiar to a solution that is not. So they create other little problems to take their minds off the big one.

Are you deliberately loosening the other legs of your table to prevent having to deal with your career issues? Are you avoiding the big, scary change? Stop, look, and listen. What is going on? Perhaps, you have to take a deep breath, face that change squarely in the eye, and go for it. Life will probably be a lot less stressful once the big challenge is off your mind.

Follow the advice in this book. Take steps each day toward discovering and having the work that you really want. Once your stress level is down and your career is back on track, you may be surprised to see enthusiasm returning to other areas of your life, as well.

## Passion Action Checklist

- ❑ I have shed attitudes and beliefs that no longer serve me.
- ❑ I have let go of old dreams that have lost their luster and am concentrating on my new ones.
- ❑ I accept compliments gracefully and am not burdening myself with perfectionism
- ❑ I take action each day toward getting my career back on track.
- ❑ I have put little changes on the back burner and am focusing on one major change—my career.

# DARE TO GO FOR IT

***In order to discover new oceans, you must have the courage to lose sight of the shore.***

André Gide

## Listen to the Bad Stuff, and Do Something.

***Put any false pride aside and look for the kernel of truth in what people offer you as feedback. Everyone has some obstacles. Winners get over them.***

There's an old ranch expression that goes something like this: *If one person calls you a horse's a**, ignore him. If two people call you a horse's a**, it's a coincidence. If three people call you a horse's a**, it's time to buy a saddle.*

People have different reactions to criticism. Some are better at receiving it than others. When people hear something negative for the first time it may jolt them a little and hurt their feelings, or they may brush it off. But when they hear things about themselves that they did not want to hear for the third, fourth or even fifth time, they often get angry. "What is wrong with these people?" "Can't they see what my real intention is?" If this is you, put your anger in your pocket, listen, and do something.

You are not the target. If someone criticizes you, it isn't about your whole personality; it is usually about only one small aspect of your behavior that is getting in your way. Listen and learn.

This true story about Beverly is a prime example of what *not* do to.

Beverly got herself a great new job working for a terrific boss. On her first day at work, however, she discovered to her surprise that he had been transferred.

Beverly noticed that she intimidated her new boss, who had much less education that she did, but she did not care. She was proud of herself, even a little arrogant, and thought that if she did a great job she would impress her boss anyway. Beverly succeeded in her project but alienated everyone in the process. She disregarded corporate culture, crossed lines of authority, and was an all-round bully.

Called into her boss's office one day, Beverly was expecting a promotion. She was fired. Why? She had not listened. Paying a little attention to what people had been saying about her intimidating, bullying style could have saved Beverly her job and quite a lot of heartache.

Take a moment and think of one critical thing that various people have told you about yourself. If you have heard the same thing three or more times, you need to pay attention.

Take a deep breath and look for the kernel of truth in the criticism. Then make a plan to do something about it. People do not expect you to have a personality transplant. You do not have to change who you are, but you *do* have to learn a new skill if you want to succeed. Be a winner. Surprise people into never having to say that critical thing to you again.

## Get Smart

***If you believe that you need more education to enhance your career, get it. It is not as scary or as difficult as you may think.***

No matter what level of education or experience people have, when facing challenges at work, they often question their own intelligence.

Donna was listening to a guest speaker (yours truly) talk about passion in the workplace.

After the talk, she sheepishly approached me and said, "You know, there is something that is holding me back in my career. I have always regretted that I never went to university. I know that I am an intelligent woman. I have a good job, but I always feel inadequate, and the lack of confidence is getting to me. I wish I had more education."

"So go back to school," I suggested. She was flabbergasted at the thought of attending university now. She said, nervously, "Well, I was never a very good student in high school, and besides, I'm almost fifty!"

I suggested that she check out her local university online, select a course or two that interested her and go talk to the professor. She nearly fell over. "Who me," she said, "talk to a *professor*? I would be *terrified*!"

I reassured her that professors were people, too, and that the person would probably be delighted to talk with her. I said that if I were a university professor and a stranger telephoned me and wanted to talk with me because my course descriptions were the most interesting in the school, it would make my day.

Three months later Donna and I met once again. In her delightful sheepish style, Donna said, "I am taking that university course." "Fabulous," I replied, "and how is it going?" "It's hard," she said, "to get the old gray matter working again. But I am passing and I have enrolled for another course. But the best part," she said with a huge smile, "is that I don't feel stupid any more. Now I know I can do it. Even if I never finish a whole degree, it doesn't matter. I've climbed over the wall."

The confidence Donna now exuded improved both her attitude toward her work and her performance appraisals. She soon applied for and received an exciting promotion.

Do you believe that lack of education is holding you back? If so, take a lesson from Donna and check out your local college or university. Review their programs and their individual courses. Decide exactly what it is that you want.

Next, check whether your company has an education plan. Many employers, anxious to keep good people, will contribute to higher education that has a professional development focus.

Do not let your concerns about education get in your way. Take one step at a time, as Donna did, and you can climb over the wall too.

## The Shortest Distance

***The education or information you need to move your career forward may require a weekend course rather than a university degree. Check it out.***

For Donna, self-esteem was the issue and it was important for her to go to university. For others, the issue could be job advancement, and university might be their answer as well. But if you are regretting not going to university or not having that extra degree to move your career forward, it is important to ask yourself whether you really need the degree to get what you want. Sometimes people only *think* they need a university degree. If it is information you require, it may be more important to choose the fastest, most efficient route.

Judith wanted to move into the business unit of her company. She was in human resources, but business excited her more. She also saw that, in that unit, she could potentially earn much more money. But she had no business experience whatsoever.

Although a university degree or college diploma might have come in handy at this point, Judith had neither the time nor the money to go back to school. Neither did she have the inclination.

So Judith got creative. She contacted the AARP, the American Association of Retired Professionals and found mentors for free. She attended free seminars at the local library. She asked friends and acquaintances for advice and she read like mad. She sought information on the internet and from the sales people in her local mega book store. They told her which business books were the hottest. Judith got the education and information that she needed quickly and at no charge.

The next time she saw an advertisement on the company bulletin board for a position in the business unit, she gathered up her courage and applied.

Because this was an internal job, Judith got the interview based on her great track record and previous performance appraisals. Even though she did not have any business experience, people were willing to at least hear her out and give her a chance. When they asked her whether she had finance experience (which she didn't), she replied craftily. "Yes," she said, confidently. "Oh?" they inquired, knowing that Judith's previous job had not involved finance. "I am a divorced mom with three children. I have been managing a budget just fine for five years now. I am sure I can do it at work. After all, it's just more zeros." She got the job.

Are you holding yourself back because something is missing from your resume? Don't let lack of experience or credentials stop you from reaching for what you want at work. Your company wants passionate, vibrant, committed employees, not bored ones. Judith's enthusiasm and willingness to learn will bring much more to the job than the company would get from someone who was qualified yet unhappy.

## Advise Your Friend, Advise Yourself

***When we see a challenge from a distance, our fear dissipates. Detach yourself from your situation and advise yourself as you might advise a friend.***

If you want to buy a new car or a piece of furniture, you do not expect the perfect one to be sitting on your doorstep when you wake up in the morning. You do your homework. You gather information, talk to people, go shopping, look at magazines and advertisements, and check out different options, as you have done for a variety of things at various times in your life. Eventually, when you have enough information, you make a decision. This may be troublesome and time-consuming, but perhaps you find a way to make it fun. Changing jobs or careers, however, is an entirely different story.

Career shift is a more frightening kind of change. Issues of power and self-esteem jump to the foreground, and these factors can cause people to stay stagnant for years. What a loss that is, for both the individual and the organization!

People do not expect the perfect sofa to find them, but they do expect some magical boss or company president to suddenly discover them, working their hearts out in their little corner of the world. It disappoints them when few seem to notice or care. The more senior people are all in *their* corners working *their* hearts out.

When people are unhappy for long periods of time, paralysis can set in. They begin to fear they could not succeed. They talk themselves into believing that "nothing is perfect" and they stay in their unhappy situation. The longer they stay, the more paralyzed they become.

People scare themselves. They see re-doing that resume as the task of a lifetime and resist it like a contagious disease. People worry about interviews when they haven't even decided what they want to do yet. All they know is that they are unhappy and do not know what to do about it.

So how to get unstuck? You can stop scaring yourself and get some distance by pretending you are giving advice to someone else. It is amazing how taking yourself out of the picture can diminish that anxiety.

If your friend came to you for advice on challenges similar to yours, what would you say to your friend? Make a list for your imaginary friend who is in the same job situation as you are. Then go a step further for your imaginary friend and take some first steps.

## Eagle or Chicken?

***Don't be "chicken" to take the next steps in your career. Stretch yourself beyond your comfort zone to reach for what you want at work.***

The actions involved in putting passion back into your paycheck will most likely require you to stretch yourself; that means you probably have to leave your comfort zone in order to get what you want. That may mean developing skills that you are not sure of, learning a language you are not comfortable with, going out and meeting people when you would rather stay behind your computer, or learning computer skills when you would rather not have to. But if you want things to change, you have to boot yourself out of your comfort zone, however painful that may be, and take action.

You may be thinking, "What does she mean, 'comfort zone'? I'm stressed to the max here. I am so far from comfort that I can't even remember how to spell the darn word. I'd give anything for some comfort right now!"

Your situation may not be comfortable, but it is familiar. There is comfort in the familiar. People use all kinds of excuses to avoid change, even when their situation is difficult. They say things like: "It's the same everywhere." "I'll get over it." "I'll learn to adjust." Corporate leaders do not want you to just "cope" they want you to do well. That is why you were hired. If you are not doing your best, you are much better off doing something else. Everyone will be better off. So don't fool yourself into believing that staying off track and unhappy at work is serving anyone. When you are less stressed and more on track at work, you and everyone around you, at work and home, will be happier. You may be holding back on taking action because change, even good change, can be scary. You are stepping into the unknown, and that is not comfortable.

You may also not have the energy. Your work may be taking so much out of you that you feel too exhausted to do anything about it once you get home.

Taking action may appear draining, but pushing yourself and taking steps to get back on track will do the opposite. It will energize you. You don't have to make any drastic changes today—you just have to build up your courage and your strength, and start doing *something*.

Think of basketball. To score, the player must reach. The same is true for hockey, football, baseball, and even tennis. In any sport, winners have to stretch both physically and mentally. They have to reach to make that shot, catch or save. And when they succeed, what exhilaration!

If you want things to be different, you have to stretch yourself too. As you move forward in your steps to bring passion back into your career, your energy level will rise. And as you reach beyond your comfort zone, you will not only become comfortable in new areas, but you will also expand your comfort zone into areas that you may never have expected.

## Passion Action Checklist

- ☐ I look for the seed of truth in criticism, learn from it, and move on.

- ☐ I am taking steps to get any education I think I need to move forward.

- ☐ I have checked out training companies to see if any of them offer short courses that will give me skills that I require.

- ☐ When I get stuck, I pretend I am advising a friend, then I take my own advice. This moves me forward.

- ☐ I stretch myself beyond my comfort zone and take positive action on my career goals.

# FOCUS YOUR ATTENTION

***If your happiness depends on what somebody else does, I guess you do have a problem.***

Richard Bach

## Find a New Perspective

***When things are not going as you wish they were and there is no change in sight, diminish your stress by learning to see the situation through new eyes.***

Mark, a federal government employee, had a very stressful job. He was leading a high profile team that was writing legislation for an inflammatory issue about which the government was vacillating. The team would work extra hours to complete a very difficult consultation with stakeholders, only to hear that the project might be cancelled. The next week the project was on again and Mark had to gear up his team once more. How could Mark keep himself and his team motivated when they never knew whether the project was going to go ahead or not? Interestingly, Mark and his team stayed motivated and relatively stress-free. What was their secret?

Mark knew that if the team members' concept of success was tied to completion of the project, they would be dejected every time the government vacillated. There was no guarantee that the project would not end up in the wastebasket.

So how did Mark get his group to care? "We created our own benchmarks," he said. "We tied off small pieces of the project and when we competed them, we celebrated. And we made it a point to learn as much as we could along the way. We actually had fun, met interesting people from outside the organization, and acquired many new skills."

Mark's group got to have "fun" in an extremely stressful work situation. This may sound incredible but it is true. I know. I was a consultant to his team.

So how does this apply to you? Keeping your stress level down and motivation up requires being willing to see things through different eyes. You may not be able to control what is going on around you, but you can notice your attitude and be willing to shift it a little.

How can you shift your perspective to view your situation differently? Perhaps you can see your situation as a learning experience? Perhaps you can change what you perceive as benchmarks of your success. If your only benchmarks of success are things that may be impossible to achieve, no wonder you are stressed! Create your own benchmarks, even if they are different from those of your team or unit. And reward yourself on their accomplishment.

Most important, if your happiness depends on somebody else doing something, you're in trouble. Learn to see your managers and colleagues through new eyes. Respect their right to have different opinions, attitudes, and work styles from you, and respect their right to think they are right.

## Pay Attention to Style

***People have different styles and priorities. Making sure you and your colleagues are on the same wavelength is an important factor in keeping your passion alive at work.***

The best way to demonstrate how matching priorities can enhance your career is to tell another true story about Marie.

Marie accepted a job that involved moving to a new city and working for John. She had heard that he was difficult to work for, but was confident that she would be able to figure him out.

Marie worked hard and created new initiatives that put her company on the international map in her field. But John fought her at every turn, neither recognizing her accomplishments nor showing appreciation. Marie was flabbergasted when, after all her hard work, she got a mediocre performance appraisal. She was clueless as to what was going on.

Marie had started the job confident that she would be able to figure her boss out, but did she? No. She flew right into doing what in her mind were great things, and expected him to be impressed. She never took the time to figure out what *he* valued. She just assumed everyone thought the same way as she did. But that is not the way people operate.

We each see the world through our own eyes and have our own value systems. Marie needed to take the time to get on her boss's wavelength. But how does one do that?

Here is a simple rule for you. When you don't know what to do, listen and observe. When we watch and listen, people show us loudly and clearly not only what they value but also how they see the world.

When Marie started paying attention, it did not take her long to see what John valued. Marie was creative and loved venturing into new territory. John liked stability. He liked to know that things were moving along smoothly, on time, and within budget. Marie realized that what she viewed as success was actually giving her boss stress!

Marie did not give up on her creativity, but she did change her approach, making sure to give John the assurances that he needed along the way. As his needs were met and his resistance diminished, Marie's stress level went down and her passion began to return.

So how does this apply to you? We are all prone to thinking that if people do not see things as we do there is something wrong with them. You need to lose that concept right now! If people around you seem obstructionist, perhaps they see the situation differently.

Take the time to observe and listen to your colleagues. Find out what they value and how they see the world. Marie's career took a giant leap forward, and yours will, too, when you ensure that you understand and take into consideration others' style.

## Read the Non-Verbals

***Only seven percent of communication has to do with actual words. Become aware and in control of the other ninety-three percent to make sure you are transmitting what you want and receiving people's words accurately.***

Research by Dr. Albert Mehrabian, professor emeritus at UCLA, tells us that communication is seven percent words, fifty-three percent body language, and thirty-eight percent tone of voice. Being in better control of your non-verbal signals and learning to read and deal with others' is a fast and easy way to significantly enhance communication and move forward in your career.

To understand this more clearly, let us look at what happened to Jessie. Jessie took pride in being a vibrant, expressive person. She was also quite transparent. Her thoughts and feelings showed through easily, and since Jessie valued honesty, she thought her transparency was a positive attribute.

One Monday morning, Jessie was called into her boss's office. Her boss was furious at Jessie for having criticized her publicly at a meeting the previous Friday. Jessie was stunned. "But I didn't say a word!" protested Jessie, who had deliberately remained silent during her boss's presentation. Her boss then looked her in the eye and said, "But your eyes went wide." Jessie's boss, rightly or wrongly, had interpreted Jessie's facial expression as one of criticism.

There are lessons here for both Jessie and her boss. Jessie needs to be more aware of the power of her expressiveness, and she needs to use it wisely and appropriately. Not speaking out publicly when you disagree with someone means being silent with your body language too. Although Jessie had not spoken, her body language had screamed disapproval, and the boss was surely not the only one who saw it.

The boss should have called Jessie on her facial expression, right in the meeting, and asked her to voice her concerns. Simply acknowledging the troubling facial expression and asking what's up, in an assertive (non-aggressive, defensive or judgmental) manner, could have surfaced and sorted the problem right on the spot, with no lingering, festering negativity

Pay attention to your non-verbal communication. Whether you are expressive, quiet or somewhere in between, you are still transmitting information. People assign meanings to your non-verbal behaviors and act as if those were what you were really thinking. Sometimes they read you correctly, sometimes incorrectly, and this, as with Jessie, can affect your career.

Tone of voice is also readable on the telephone and in e-mail. Be aware. People are always picking up meanings. You need to make sure you are transmitting what you want others to receive, and reading correctly what others send.

## Clean the Filters

***Everything people perceive gets filtered through a "personal historian," an internal recorder of all past experiences. If your "historian" is getting in the way of your success, pay attention and do something.***

Dan had a serious problem working with people who had red hair. It was affecting his relationships with management, colleagues, and especially with clients. He did not know why, but red haired people made his skin crawl and the hair stand up on the back of his neck. What was it, he wondered, about red-haired people that made them so disgusting to him? Dan realized he could not go through the rest of his life unable to work with people who had red hair so he decided to stop, look, and listen—to himself and his reactions.

Then an idea hit him like a bolt out of the blue. His father had had red hair, and his father had been a rather brutal man. At some instinctive level, Dan's "personal historian" had recorded the information that red-haired people were dangerous.

Once Dan made the connection, although he might still have a gut reaction to red-haired people, he could put this reaction into its proper place, back in his own childhood. He could deal with red-haired individuals as people unto themselves, not as shadows of his late father.

If certain people irritate you, you can gauge how much your "personal historian" is involved by the level of your reaction. If your colleague Joe is aggravating, put your reaction on an imaginary Richter scale. If Joe rates a two, three or even four on your scale, Joe may just be an irritating person. He probably rubs many people the wrong way.

But if Joe really gets to you, and your reaction is a seven or eight on the Richter scale, then you can bet that your "personal historian" has recognized something familiar and perhaps threatening about Joe, and that "something" has more to do with your past than with Joe.

Is there someone whom you find infuriating, frightening, or threatening? Is there someone whom you have written off and want nothing to do with? If this person is seriously dangerous, then you have certainly made a wise decision, but if this is a colleague at work, you may want to rethink the situation.

Everyone has filters and baggage. Successful people recognize them and move on. Doing the Richter scale test will help you sort out which of your reactions are coming from the present and which from the past, and prevent these past fears from interfering with your success. Like Dan, you may always have some level of reaction to that person, but that reaction will be cut down to a manageable size, and will no longer be able to interfere with your career, cause you stress, and dampen your spirit.

## The Aikido Focus

***Channel negative energy into positive actions that move you forward.***

In Aikido, a Japanese martial art, rather than trying to block the opponent's energy, the fighter blends with it and uses that energy to bring the opponent down. If two people are fighting each other in the Western way, all a person has is his or her own energy, which is great if the person is very strong. Aikido uses the combined energy of both people to the fighter's advantage. Double the power, with less effort—sounds great, doesn't it?

If your stress level is high at work and you find yourself in the grip of strong emotions, one solution is to use the lesson from Aikido. Channel the energy into something positive. Another story about Marie provides a good example. Marie could do nothing to change her situation and she felt powerless. But she was giving so much energy to being angry, frustrated, and feeling like a victim that she had none left to think and plan.

One evening, furious and in pain, Marie began to write about her frustrations at work. A few hours later, she reread what she had written, and there was the chapter outline for a full book. She sat back, dumbfounded. Where had all this energy come from? It had sprung from the anger and she had redirected it. That was when she realized the real power of emotion. She found that the trick was to get behind that power and go with it.

Think of a revolving door. How do you enter a revolving door? The distance may seem shorter if you were to enter the door sooner and push it in the opposite direction. But you would not think of doing that. You know how easy it is to keep the door moving once it has started, and you go in the direction the door is moving. But you had to learn that. A child entering a revolving door for the first time has to be taught. If people's emotions are like that revolving door, and they go with the energy, rather than fight it, they get through.

When you feel anger or frustration at work, don't fight it; use it. You may not be a writer like Marie. Jared wasn't either. But their frustration led them to plan what they wanted and go for it. Channel your powerful emotions into positive directions. Use the energy to help you take the steps you need to get back on track and move forward.

## Passion Action Checklist

- ❑ I am willing to change my perspective and see things and people through new eyes.

- ❑ I pay attention to my colleagues' style and present information to them in ways they can understand.

- ❑ I am aware of my non-verbal communication and do not make assumptions about others'.

- ❑ I pay attention when I have strong reactions to people and things and can separate what is mine from what is theirs.

- ❑ I channel negative emotions into positive actions.

# LISTEN, THEN SPEAK

***Talking is like playing on the harp; there is as much in laying the hands on the strings to stop their vibration as in twanging them to bring out their music.***

Oliver Wendell Holmes

## Listen is an Action Word

***Multi-tasking is rampant and often necessary, but to hear the full message, you need to stop and pay attention, and ask people to listen to you in return. Being a good listener is a valuable tool in moving your career forward.***

If someone is speaking and you are not listening, they can tell immediately. They will get agitated and more vocal and take double the time they would have taken had they known you were listening. You also may think you hear them, but you don't, really, and it shows.

Stop what you are doing, give the person full eye contact and full attention, nod a little, add a few uh-huhs, ask or answer a simple question or two, and they will probably finish what they were saying, solve their problem, and disappear in a few minutes. They are most likely just as busy as you are.

If they go on speaking too long and you only have five minutes, say so, and stick to it. But be silent and attentive during those five minutes.

If you are really busy and have no time at all, tell the other person, and arrange for a time when you *can* listen, and specify the length of time; for example, suggest meeting at 3:00 p.m. for fifteen minutes. Then be there, and listen.

There are times, however, when you may have to do more than just listen. To advance in your career and be perceived as a valuable asset, you must be able to sort what is yours to do and what is not, and take action where appropriate.

In simple terms, if someone comes to you with a problem and you think they just need to vent, listen and they will probably blow off steam and move on within five minutes. If, however, they come to you with something that is yours to solve, you need to listen well and find a way to solve it on the spot or fit it into your schedule.

Know, too, that when people are very emotional about their problems, they will not be able to hear any solutions you offer. They need to calm down first. The best thing you can do when people are emotional, providing they are not abusive, is to listen attentively for a few minutes, show them you care (even if you do not agree with them—they are upset so now is not the time to tell them you disagree), tell them you see that is important to them and that you will give it some thought and get back to them. This will calm down their emotions and give them some cooling down time. When you get back to them, they will have calmed down somewhat and be more logical.

Conversely, if you have something important to say to someone, ask politely for the time that you need. If the person is busy and it is not a dire emergency, tell the person how much time you will need and ask him or her to set a time later.

Also, do not try to solve your problem when you are upset. Vent first—on paper, which you later throw out, to a trusted friend, or by going for a walk, or getting a coffee or juice. After you calm down, you will be better able to find solutions yourself. If not, and you must go to others for solutions, they will be able to pay much more attention when not distracted by your emotion.

Stressful times at work are challenging to our emotions. Being able to deal with your emotions, and listen attentively to others without distraction is a valuable key to staying on track.

## Not Now, Colette

***You are not the company shrink. To keep your spirits up at work, take care of yourself when people come to you with their emotional problems. To prevent others from dragging you down, tell them that you are too busy to listen.***

Unfortunately, as we have discovered, some people find a problem that is familiar more comfortable than a solution that isn't. They just like to complain. Moreover, you may not be in a position to listen at that moment. Perhaps you know someone like Colette.

Colette kept interrupting her colleague to complain about her boyfriend. He was not what she wanted in a variety of ways. She was considering breaking up with him and it was only a matter of time. One day she was particularly upset. *He* had broken up with *her* and she was devastated.

Tired of hearing her complain without being willing to do anything about it, Colette's colleague tried just listening without offering solutions. But Collette didn't calm down and, finding a good listener, kept returning and interrupting.

The colleague decided it was time to put a little space between herself and Collette, so she avoided lunch with her by eating at her desk or going for a run at noon, and apologized for being too busy to listen when Collette tried to interrupt her at her desk. This may seem cruel, but Collette was really getting her down and interfering with her work.

A few months later, Collette changed her tune. She had answered an ad in the personals and met the man of her dreams. Well, what do you know? Collette got over her problem herself. She didn't need her colleague to do it.

Sometimes you are too busy or are not in the mood to listen. Anyone who knows you well enough will understand and find someone else to talk to. All parties will be much better off if you say politely, "Sorry, not now, Colette," rather than listen resentfully.

There are also limits to how much discussion of personal problems is appropriate in the workplace. Colleagues will discuss personal issues to a certain degree, but when a complaining colleague is bringing you down or getting in the way of your doing your job, it is not okay. It is much better, both for you and the colleague, if you say that you cannot listen.

## Ask and You Shall Receive

***To move forward in your career you need to ask for what you want. This requires clarity, both mentally and verbally. Get it on paper, get it into your mind, then get it into your mouth. Write it, see it, then say it.***

If you have read the previous points in this book, you have some ideas about what will put passion back into your paycheck and what may be getting in your way. Now you need to ask for what you want, but you must be clear. The first step is to get it on paper.

When you approach your boss, team lead or colleagues about what you want to do, you do not want to fumble or mumble and expect them to fill in the blanks. They are not mind readers. They are busy with their own concerns and not necessarily tuned in to what you might want.

Any significant project requires four times more time for planning than for execution. Putting passion back into your career is a serious project. Take the required time to plan. Get down on paper exactly what you want, why you want it, and how it will further team, unit, departmental, or organizational goals. Do some research, anticipate potential questions, and prepare answers. Think about creating a win-win situation. Be ready to show how doing what you want will meet corporate goals as well as your own. Plan to present your research in a way that will resonate with your boss. If he or she is a big picture person, focus on the big picture. If he or she is a detail person, make sure to include the details. You do not need to convince yourself; you already know what you want. You need to convince the other person. Prepare your case in a format appropriate to your listener.

After you have done your planning and prepared your case on how doing what you want would benefit your organization, it is time to use the power of your mind. Olympic athletes see themselves completing that perfect dive, run or ski in their minds many times before doing it for real. As a matter of fact, visualization is so important that it is a compulsory element in their training. If you want to be a winner, do as the athletes do. Make visualization a part of your preparation. See yourself having that conversation with your boss. Visualize yourself confident and assertive and receiving a positive response. Imagine yourself happily doing what you want at work.

Now that you have written down what you want and visualized it happening, it is time to ask for it.

How you ask is critical. Don't catch your boss on the fly while he or she is beside a colleague's cubicle or in the cafeteria. Make an appointment, bring a printout of your prepared case, and present yourself strongly, and confidently and assertively.

## Be Assertive

***Being assertive means asking for what you want in a clear, direct manner, without violating the rights of others.***

If you are to present your case strongly, confidently, and assertively, let us take a few moments to define exactly what we mean by assertive.

The word "assertive" has gotten a bit of a bad reputation lately and has become synonymous with "aggressive." To clarify the difference, let's look at four main communication styles: passive, aggressive, passive-aggressive, and assertive.

Passive behavior is quiet and withdrawn. People use this behavior when they are unwilling or unable to take a stand. There is a time and place for passive behaviour; such as when a police officer stops you for speeding, but if you behave passively most of the time at work, you will not be successful in getting what you want.

Aggressive behavior is usually associated with bullying, but its definition is much broader. Aggressive actions can be quiet and involve only a look, but boy, what a look! The key aspect of aggressiveness is that it creates negative feelings in the target person. If you treat others, even silently, in a way that makes them feel small, intimidated, angry, guilty, or frightened, you may win the battle but you will lose the war. You may get what you want in the short term, but you will get a bad reputation and your career will suffer.

Passive-aggressive behavior combines the worst of both worlds. This behaviour involves behaving passively by not dealing with a situation directly; yet getting back at the person in an underhanded manner. The target person then feels strong negative emotions, but can do nothing about them.

Let us look at an example to walk through all previous definitions. Joe is asked by his boss to take on an additional project when his schedule is already too full. Passive Joe would sheepishly take on the project. Aggressive Joe would argue about it, or agree to take it on with a sneering, nasty tone of voice—designed to make the boss feel bad. Passive aggressive Joe would say nothing, take on the project, but intentionally sabotage it behind the bosses back, either in words or deeds or both.

Now let us look at what assertive Joe would do. Assertive Joe would ask for what he wants in a clear, direct manner, without violating his boss's right to get the job done.

Assertive Joe would say, "Let me give this some thought, I'll get back to you later today." Then he would get his facts straight about all the other projects he has on hand, put the information onto a spread sheet, and make an appointment with his boss.

At the meeting, Joe would, in a clear, calm, direct manner, supported by facts, have a rational conversation with his boss. His objective would be to get his needs met, while not violating the boss's right to have needs as well. Although Joe may still end up doing some of the project, he will have made his boss aware of the implications. He will also feel much better having stood up for himself and neither burying nor harboring negative emotions. Lastly, he will be building his reputation as someone who deals wisely with difficult situations.

So what about you? It is all right to be passive sometimes, but you want to avoid being either aggressive or passive-aggressive. If you are upset about something, it is difficult to be assertive. You need to calm down first. Take the time, calm down, get your facts straight, and express yourself assertively. To emphasize what that means, here is the definition again. Being assertive means to ask for what you want in a clear, direct manner, without violating the rights of others.

## Passion Action Checklist

- ❑ I listen attentively when people are speaking and do not interrupt with possible solutions. I also ensure that people take the time to listen to me.

- ❑ When I do not have time to listen, I tell people so politely and, if I want to, set a more convenient time.

- ❑ I become clear on what I want before I speak. Then I ask for it calmly and confidently.

- ❑ I am assertive rather than passive, aggressive or passive aggressive with others.

# LEAD

*"Come to the edge," he said.*
**They said: "We are afraid."**
**"Come to the edge,"he said.**
**They came. He pushed them,**
**and they flew.**

Guillaume Apollinaire

## Provide Strong, Committed, Visionary Leadership

***Leaders need vision, goals, objective measures, and a strategy to help the group hang in when the going gets rough. All of these can reduce stress and keep motivation higher for both you and your team.***

You read early in this book about developing a vision for yourself. If you are to lead others, you need to have a vision for them too. You need a clear vision of what your group needs to accomplish. But vision is not enough.

Vision needs to be supported with goals, objectives and specific activities. You do not need to develop all of these yourself. If you create goals and objectives for all of the members of your group, you may fall into the trap of micro-managing. People do much better when they are encouraged to set their own goals and objectives. As leader, you are responsible for the bigger picture. You can have goals and objectives for yourself, but encourage your people to set their own as well.

If you know what you want your team to accomplish and, together, you have set goals and objectives, how will you gauge how well they are progressing toward those goals? People do well when they have a sense of accomplishment. As Mark did earlier in this book, if your project is complex, tie off pieces and celebrate when these are completed. This creates some light at the end of the tunnel and keeps motivation up.

If you are leading people, you have to have strategies in the back of your mind to keep spirits up, both yours and theirs, when the going gets rough. This can often be the most challenging aspect when leading others. It can be difficult enough to keep one's own spirits up during challenging times, let alone encourage others.

You know right now what you do to lift your spirits. What is it? Do you go for a run, watch a TV show, talk to a friend, play golf? What do you do that always makes you feel better?

Clearly you can't go off in the middle of a strenuous meeting and play a round of golf. Neither can you turn on your favourite TV show. But it is important to take time outside of work to recharge your batteries. The fun *after* work will make you more effective *at* work.

In addition, here is a psychological trick that can keep your spirits up. Imagine you are playing golf. This may sound silly but it really does work. Your mind has more power than you think. If you take five minutes and imagine really well, you can fool your body into producing endorphins. Before you write this off as unrealistic, try it right now for a couple of minutes. See yourself doing something you really enjoy. I'll bet you a free book that a smile comes to your face. When you can keep your spirits up, you are better able to keep others' spirits up too.

## Ensure Equality and Respect for All

***Respect and value individuals regardless of their occupation, gender, culture, or place on the organizational chart. Creative teamwork and co-operative problem solving across corporate, gender, and cultural lines are absolutely essential to keep passion alive and people on track.***

Demonstrating equality and respect for others at work is a sure sign of a great leader, especially since one has to do it on many levels. The leader must suspend personal judgments and support all members of the team. Let's look first at occupational differences.

A common challenge is the relationship between technicians and salespeople. Salespeople can set deadlines that technicians find impossible. Technicians can provide reports that salespeople find unintelligible. Respect involves being willing to see the situation through other people's eyes, communicating in a language other people can understand, being willing to listen to and value their concerns, and working cooperatively toward solutions.

Technical people often put detailed information into their reports because that is what they need to understand the situation or solve the problem. They can disrespect others, who may not be as technical, for not understanding or belittling the value of the information. When technical people realize that others require much less in their reports, it can be a relief. Learning to value what others need to see, not what they themselves need to show, can reduce workload as well as increase communication and reduce stress.

It is the leader's responsibility to facilitate that communication, without judgment. The salespeople are not stupid because they do not understand technical things. The technical people are not stupid because they do not understand the ins and outs of marketing and sales. A good leader values the contributions of all members of the team and helps team members to value one another.

Valuing people regardless of gender or sexual orientation has been an important issue in the workplace for a while now. Good leaders ensure that they deal with any of their own personal biases and do not let inappropriate attitudes or behavior interfere with team success. This, of course, applies to culture as well.

The degree of diversity in our workplaces is astounding. This calls on the leader to help team members respect and value one another regardless of race, religion, or nationality. The good leader helps team members to respect cultural needs, to include everyone, and also to not make assumptions. With openness and respect, common interests and goals bind people together and minimize cultural differences.

Lastly, people at all levels on the organizational chart deserve to be treated respectfully. If you lead wisely and do not tolerate bigotry, your team will function at a much higher level.

No section on equality and respect would be complete without a few words on teasing. Teasing is *not* funny. You may be thinking, "How can she say that? We kid each other all the time. It's part of our culture here." Well, be wise and change your culture. Teasing can take a nosedive very quickly, and you will have a harassment complaint on your hands. Your Human Resources department can tell you unhappy stories of teasing that went bad.

Something said at others' expense is never funny. They may laugh it off and seem the good sport, but one day someone will step over the line, feelings will be hurt, stress will rise, and the project will suffer.

Be a leader. Set the tone of equality and respect for others regardless of occupation, gender, culture, or place on the organizational chart, and stop the teasing.

## Share Information Up, Down, and Sideways

***If you have information that others need in order do their jobs better, make sure they get it. Timely access to information helps people stay on track and reduces stress.***

To do their best, people need quick and direct access to information affecting them and their work. They need to know as much as possible about upcoming organizational changes and they certainly need information that affects their clients.

These stories about Joseph and Russell demonstrate the value of having up-to-date, accurate information.

The first line of customer interface at his work, Joseph was a bank teller. While participating in a national study on client service, he said to the consultant: "Clients come in asking about this particular new account that they saw advertised in the newspaper and I know nothing about it. Then I have to scramble around, asking my colleagues if they have heard of it and they don't know anything either. It is so embarrassing!"

The consultant determined that a critical missing element in that bank's customer service was their tellers' lack of speedy access to up-to-date product information. As a result of her report, the bank put in many changes including a new program to ensure that tellers were among the first to know about product changes and enhancements.

Information must flow up as well as down.

Russell, a biologist, also part of a study, told a frustrating story about how an external consultant was hired, at great expense, to do an environmental project that an internal committee had been working on for quite some time. Somehow that information had not gotten up the line to the managers who needed to know about it.

So what does this have to do with you? Leaders need to ensure that information gets transmitted in all directions, up, down, and sideways. Make sure that the appropriate senior people have the information they need in order to make decisions that relate to your projects. Provide your team and the people below them with the information that they require to do their jobs as efficiently as possible, and ensure that important parallel teams also stay in the loop. That will enable them to provide your team members with what they need in return.

Sharing information is a critical element in keeping others on track and keeping passion alive at work. Find ways to share timely information with everyone who needs it.

## Value People, Learn from Mistakes

***Show appreciation and refrain from blame. Valuing people keeps spirits up and is like money in the bank. Valued people, who are not victimized when things go wrong, will rise to the occasion during difficult times.***

Stefanie had a poster on her cubicle wall. It showed a droopy-eyed dog and the following caption: "When I am good, no one remembers. When I am bad, no one forgets."

Many people are like Stefanie. Their spirits are lifted when their contributions are acknowledged. This does not mean you have to wave a flag and throw a party. People just want to go home at the end of the day thinking that their time on the job makes a difference; that they are not just robots or cogs in a wheel. People like to think that if they dropped dead on the job, someone would notice.

Leaders need to show their people, with words—and particularly with actions—a degree of appreciation. Smile. Say thank-you. Buy the team a box of doughnuts once in a while.

Martin takes valued employees to an NHL hockey game. At one company, employees who make their sales targets get to spend four days in the Bahamas. Marcia in California has a business called the Corporate Fairy Godmother. Companies hire her when they want to create a special reward day for staff.

Some of these rewards may be a little over your budget, but doughnuts aren't. There is always something you can do. One company requires employees who receive awards to buy doughnuts for their team. That is an ingenious solution that can go a long way to minimize jealousy.

Conversely, it is particularly important for you to allow, even expect, people to make mistakes once in a while. People learn from mistake. Edison did not invent the light bulb on the first try.

In summary, take the time to show your people some appreciation. There is no need to get syrupy about it. A simple smile and a nod can get people through a difficult day. When troubles surface, rather than blaming, assume that people have been doing their best and take a problem-solving approach. When people feel valued, they rise to the occasion and participate readily in finding solutions.

## Hire the Expertise, then Use It

***Go the extra mile to find the right person for the job, and don't forget to use their expertise once you have it.***

You need to do your absolute best to put the right people into the right jobs. People find it difficult to stay passionate about their work when they do not respect the person above them. Sometimes this can be difficult. Internal hires can be easier and cheaper than external ones, but finding the right person must come first.

James had the courage to be patient until the right person came along. He was setting up a new unit. His current assistant yearned for the much more professional and higher paying job that was being created. "I am really feeling pressured," he confided to a colleague. "She could probably do the job, barely. But I want someone who is familiar with the work we will be doing, someone who can teach *me*, who can take this unit to the next level."

It took James six months of lobbying management and interviewing candidates, but he held his ground and finally prevailed. He hired someone who has the qualifications he was seeking. On the other side of the coin, people tend, unfortunately, to take the familiar for granted. Leaders need to stay informed and use the expertise they have within the organization before spending money on consultants.

People love to be the experts they are. It fuels their energy, their passion, and nourishes their need to make a difference. Leaders bring out the best in people when they give them the opportunity to use all of their talents and skills. And it is good for the company too—both professionally and financially.

So how does this apply to you? If you are in a position to hire people or select members for a team, do whatever you can to put the right person into the job. Make every effort not to cater to any political pressure to settle for less. Do your homework, get data, and convince people if you have to. The time spent up front will save time later.

And don't forget to use the expertise you already have around you. People get extremely turned off when their talents and skills are ignored. Paying attention to and using these people can avoid their becoming angry and potentially sabotaging the project down the road.

## Listen

***Develop your listening skills and your patience. If you listen attentively, people will find creative solutions to thorny problems—solutions that might never have occurred to you—and feel exhilarated in the process.***

Leadership requires having good listening and questioning skills. It is difficult to learn to listen without judgment, and challenging to learn to ask the right questions. Leaders are often so concerned about having to provide answers that they do not listen long enough to get the full picture. Sometimes they even shut down on hearing bad news and say, "Come to me with solutions, not problems!"

It is important to be able to listen, particularly when something is going wrong. You must also learn to listen longer, to ask good questions and provide guidance, without taking over the problem.

As discussed earlier, people will often solve their own problems if you give them a little time and don't jump in and try to solve their problem for them. Trouble is, you probably want them to process information *your* way.

Others see the world through their own eyes, not through yours. You need to remember who owns the problem. When you take over other people's problems and work at solving them yourself, you take away their power and diminish their self-esteem.

Children as young as five-years-old solve problems. Parents of toddlers can tell you that problem solving starts even earlier. By the time people reach adulthood, what a wealth of problem solving experience they have acquired!

So, when others come to you with problems or propose strange-sounding solutions, listen without judgment, help them ask themselves good questions, and let them continue problem solving on their own. Working through a thorny problem provides opportunities to learn, and discovering solutions stimulates passion and enthusiasm.

## Go for the Gusto

***Take responsibility. Do your part to inspire and bring out the best in others by making sure you do what is yours to do.***

You must not take on responsibilities that belong to others, but you cannot shrink from your own responsibilities either. Sometimes it is difficult to know where to draw the line. Find your answer by going back to basics. If there is a corporate issue that is getting in the way of the job, it is the manager's or team lead's responsibility to fix it; to get the brambles out of the way so that workers can have a clear path to do the job. The work is the employees', but the corporate battles belong to the leader.

Here is a perfect example. Jamie was a human resources professional in an organization that was about to undergo a merger. "Nobody will tell us what is going on," lamented Jamie. "There will be duplicate human resource services when we merge and nobody is deciding who will do what to whom! We are just being told to call our counterparts at the other organization and work it out ourselves. Who the heck is in charge here?"

Understandably, Jamie's manager felt powerless too. He did not know what was going on either and was waiting for corporate direction, but he still needed to do something! He didn't and it had devastating consequences. His people got angry and took it out on each other. The infighting undermined any work that they had to get done in the year that preceded the actual merger.

So what could you do in a case like this, a case where you may not have total power but you do have responsibility; when people are asking you questions to which you may not have the answers?

When the going gets tough at sea, captains don't let go of the wheel. They hang on and steer the ship through. The manager could have met with his counterpart at the other organization and had some preliminary discussions. He also could have told the staff the truth and encouraged them to wait until things sorted a bit and he got clearer direction from above. In any case, he could have done something to manage and quell the fears of his people so work could proceed in the meantime.

When people come to you with a problem, ask yourself, "Is this mine to solve?" If it is, go for it. If not, help people to find the tools to solve the problem themselves.

## Fix the Mismatch

***If you inherit people who don't fit, be patient. Take the time to figure out what they are good at and what they value so you can get them on track. If this proves impossible, find a place where they can succeed.***

If you inherit people who don't fit your needs, take the time to figure out how they *can* fit in. They must have been good at something or they probably would have been fired before you got there. To shed light on this section, here is a challenge that Marie faced in her first managerial position back in the early '90s.

Marie inherited an administrative assistant named Jean. Jean had held that job for twenty-five years and had gotten excellent performance appraisals. She was a fantastic executive secretary. She took dictation, typed letters, answered the telephone, and made travel arrangements for her boss's many business trips. Marie arrived with her laptop, PDA, and voicemail. To her, Jean was a fossil. This was a government department so firing Jean was not an option. Besides, Jean had twenty-five years of excellent references behind her. What was Marie to do? She gave the matter some thought and came up with what *she* wanted from Jean.

Marie needed Jean to improve her proficiency in Microsoft Word and Excel and to set up a small resource library. She had conversations with Jean, put these two items into her job description and sent Jean on appropriate training.

Weeks went by. Jean's skills did not improve and the resources stayed in boxes. What was Marie to do? Eventually, she realized that Jean was not going to change. Unable to fire her, Marie had to be creative. Discussing the matter with a colleague, she came up with a solution. The colleague needed

Jean. Giving up the resource to her colleague freed room in Marie's budget to hire a summer student who was able to do exactly want Marie wanted. This true story was more than a win-win situation. It was a five-way win situation. Marie got the help she needed, her colleague got the administrative support that she needed, Jean got to do a job that she was comfortable with, the organization got its work done more efficiently, and a highly qualified university student got a summer job.

So how can this apply to you? Don't settle for mismatches on your team. There must be something you can do. If the person isn't dong the work, they probably have a good reason. Take the time to find out what the reason is. Take the time to see it from their side. Jean was two years to retirement and very uncomfortable with computer skills. She was also not a self-starter. Setting up a resource library was beyond the scope of what she believed she was capable of doing. Asking her to do what Marie wanted, even with training, was like asking a dog to say meow.

Fix the mismatches, either by providing training or arranging changes. You, and your organization, have the right to as efficient a team as possible. Think, be creative, talk to colleagues. You and your team will have a better chance of staying on track and keeping passion alive by making sure you fix any inherited mismatches.

## Give Them the Tools

***People function best and stay on track when they have the tools they need to do the job—material resources, staff, appropriate decision-making authority, and realistic time frames.***

To keep people on track and passionate about their work, they need the tools to do the job. Acquiring and providing these tools is part of what was referred to earlier as "getting the brambles out of the way." It is a required—though sometimes difficult and complex—part of the manager's or team lead's job. There are four different kinds of tools.

People need *material resources* including appropriate budget, equipment, and information. If your people need to see a certain report, make sure that they get it. If they need certain computer programs, do your best to get them. And be very meticulous when doing your budget. Your people need to see that you are expending time and energy to go to bat for the resources they need. Even if you don't get everything you are asking for, the mere attempt will go a long way to keeping them motivated.

Second, people need *appropriately trained and available human resources*. They need staff! There are many cases, particularly during budget crunches, in which people have to do not only their own jobs but also the jobs of their departed managers or colleagues. In these cases, and others in which there are not enough trained people to do the job, people get stressed and exhausted. In the long run, this does the project more harm the good. Money spent up front on appropriate staff is money well spent. Fight the battle and get the people.

Third, people require an *adequate level of decision-making authority*. One of the biggest demotivators in organizations is having responsibility without the authority to do what needs to be done. As a leader, you may need to let go and pass on some of your responsibilities. Make a realistic assessment of what you can let go of, take a deep breath, and hand it off. People have a much better chance of staying motivated and performing well when they can make or at least influence decisions affecting their work.

The last critical tool in keeping people motivated and on track is *realistic deadlines*. This is very common challenge for technical professionals who struggle with the constant dichotomy between doing it on time or doing it right. This can be a difficult situation for a team leader. Do what you can—and assure your people that you have done your best, even if you have not succeeded one hundred percent—to ensure that deadlines are as realistic as possible.

In summary, you can reduce stress and keep your people more motivated by providing the four tools they need: resources (including information), staff, an appropriate level of decision-making authority, and realistic deadlines.

## Stay Balanced—Create Eagles

***Deal with any insecurity that prevents you from encouraging others to be all they can be and bring their best to work. You may one day find that you have been a mentor to someone great.***

Leaders must find ways to keep themselves balanced and on track, particularly when faced with powerful, talented employees. Some of you may wonder why this is a problem, but others will understand. Leading potential leaders requires both skill and humility.

One of the biggest leadership challenges is the belief that one has to be smarter, faster, and more informed than the people below. This myth can cause undue stress on both leader and team.

Having to lead people smarter, faster, and better educated than you are is a fact of corporate life and it can be scary. It can cause leaders to clam up in fear, and over-manage people. Team members can then become fearful as well, and paralyzed as they worry more about pleasing their manager than about bringing their best to the job. They become chickens rather than eagles.

Marie, as you may remember, did not feel valued by her boss. To make matters worse, she then hired Lisa. On paper and during the interview, Lisa was fantastic. But she had more education than Marie, and was really smart. Marie became convinced that Lisa was after her job.

Managers who are afraid of their employees can either consciously or unconsciously try to hold them back. When Lisa told Marie she was holding her back, Marie nearly fainted from shock. "Who, me?" she thought, "Holding someone back? Impossible. I would never do that." But in her fear and insecurity, she had been.

Marie had to learn to get herself out of the way, to deal with her insecurities and find a way to bring her best to the job, while also encouraging Lisa to bring her best too.

Marie rose to the occasion. She was able to sort which challenges stemmed from her personal insecurities and which had to do with Lisa herself, who brought challenges of her own.

She took a few deep breaths and calmed herself down. Then she asked Lisa about her career aspirations, and whether or not Lisa one day hoped to manage the unit. Lisa reassured her that she absolutely did not. She preferred to stay operational and rise professionally. Lisa was very uncomfortable managing people. Whew! You see, all this time, Marie was making herself crazy over nothing. By discussing what Lisa really wanted to do, the two of them were able to collaborate in discovering a special project that would satisfy Lisa's need to develop professionally and would not compete with Marie.

To create eagles, you need to be an eagle yourself. You need to be willing to discover your mission, get your blocks out of the way, and soar. You then need to do everything you can to push others to soar also, to be their absolute best, even if that means that one day they will soar higher than you.

## Passion Action Checklist

- ❑ I have a vision, goals, objective measures, and a strategy to help the group hang in when the going gets rough.

- ❑ I respect and value individuals regardless of their occupation, gender, culture, or place on the organizational chart.

- ❑ I share information ASAP so people can do their jobs as efficiently as possible.

- ❑ I show appreciation and refrain from blame. I see mistakes as an opportunity for learning.

- ❑ I go the extra mile to find the right person for the job, and I don't forget to use the expertise once I have it.

- ❑ I continuously refine and use my listening skills and am patient.

- ❑ I take responsibility. I do my part to inspire and bring out the best in others by making sure I do what is mine to do.

- ❑ If I inherit people who don't fit, I take the time to figure them out and get them on track.

- ❑ I strive to give people the tools they need to do the job—material resources, staff, appropriate decision-making authority, and realistic time frames.

- ❑ I deal with any insecurity that prevents me from encouraging others to be all they can be. I create Eagles.

# Conclusion

You have now learned thirty-five strategies to put passion back into your paycheck. You have ideas. You have solutions. The good news is that you do not have to use them all at once.

Stop, look, and listen. Take your time and take charge. In your hands are the tools to reclaim your career and your life.

Use these strategies and you will soon find yourself less stressed, encouraged, back on track, and moving forward.

Good luck!

# Acknowledgements

This book would not have been possible without the sound advice and encouragement of Matthew Bennett of BTDT Enterprises. Matthew was, and continues to be, a fantastic inspiration and coach on all aspects of this book. Thank you, Matthew.

Thanks to Karen Opas Lanouette for her editorial expertise. Karen, you are terrific.

Thanks to Donald Lanouette for his cover design and formatting excellence. Writing is a pleasure when I know that Donald will make it shine. Thanks, Donald.

And last of all, thanks to the many wonderful people whose stories bring the strategies in this book to life. You have made all the difference.

## About the Author

With a PhD in Adult Education and Psychology from the University of Toronto, Serena Williamson has more than twenty years experience leading, advising, coaching, training, and counselling many thousands of people at all levels from a wide variety of organizations.

Dr. Williamson is the author of numerous books and CDs, which inspire people and give them the tools to thrive through challenges and be their best.

She currently resides in Ottawa, Canada.

# The Passion and the Paycheck Training

You can take Dr. Serena Williamson home.

If you find that the strategies in this book have been helpful to you and your people and would like more, Dr. Serena offers seminars and coaching programs tailored to your needs.

**Find out more at**
**www.SerenaWilliamson.com**

www.ingramcontent.com/pod-product-compliance
Lightning Source LLC
Chambersburg PA
CBHW030323070426
42446CB00048B/747